THE SOLITARY JOURNEY

The Solitary Journey

BUDDHIST MYSTICAL REFLECTIONS

edited and with photographs by
CATHARINE HUGHES

A CROSSROAD BOOK
THE SEABURY PRESS • NEW YORK

ACKNOWLEDGMENTS

Buddhist Texts Through the Ages, edited by Edward Conze. Bruno Cassirer Ltd., under the auspices of The Royal India, Pakistan and Ceylon Society, 1954.
The Gospel of Buddha, compiled by Paul Carus. The Open Court Publishing Company, 1915.
Some Sayings of the Buddha, translated by F. L. Woodward. Introduction by Christmas Humphreys. Copyright © 1973 by the Oxford University Press Ltd. Reprinted by permission of the publisher.
Texts from the Buddhist Canon, translated by Samuel Beal. Trubner and Company, 1878.

Designed by Joseph Vesely

Library of Congress Cataloging in Publication Data

Hughes, Catharine   comp.
    The solitary journey: Buddhist mystical reflections.

    "A Crossroad book."
    1. Buddha and Buddhism.   2. Mysticism—Buddhism.
I. Title.
BQ4022.H8   294.3'4'42   74-13780
ISBN 0-8164-2103-X

The wisdom and mysticism of the East have very much to give us even though they speak their own language which it is impossible to imitate. They should remind us of that which is familiar in our own culture and which we have already forgotten, and we should direct our attention to that which we have put aside as insignificant, namely the fate of our own inner man.

—Carl G. Jung

INTRODUCTION

Among the Eastern religions, Buddhism has achieved the greatest acceptance and popularity in the West. It has even been enshrined on film, with the 1973 motion picture *Siddhartha,* based on Hermann Hesse's novel, in which, as the promotion pieces put it, a "young Brahmin journeys through life in search of truth."

But Buddhism's appeal goes beyond cult or fashion, beyond any attempt to exploit it. Although it suggests that there is not an individual ego, self, or soul—in the Western sense—only a constantly changing "aggregate of energies," it possesses numerous points of contact with Western religion and thought, which undoubtedly have made it more accessible, less obscure, to Westerners than, for instance, Sufism, the mysticism of Islam, or even Taoism, which, primarily because of Lao Tzu's *Tao Te Ching* ("The Way"), has acquired an increasing number of adherents in the West.

There are, however, major differences, and it would not be altogether desirous to follow too far the assertion of the great Vedantist Swami Vivekananda, who on a visit to the West in the late nineteenth century, said: "I accept all the religions of the past and I worship God with every one of them. Can God's book be finished? Must it not be a continuing revelation? Difference is the first sign of thought. I pray that the sects may multiply until at last there will be as many sects as human beings." A bit excessive, perhaps, but as both Eastern and Western religions have acknowledged, there are times when it may not be a bad idea to *feel* rather than think. Feeling is essential to Buddhism, though "reason" also plays its role.

Buddhism is the religion of approximately one-fifth of mankind. Founded by Siddhartha Guatama, the "historic" Buddha, it is the dominant religious influence in China, Korea, Japan, Ceylon, Vietnam, Tibet, Mongolia, and a number of other Asian countries. Wherever it has had a religious affect, there has been a parallel artistic and social one and Buddhist sculpture, iconography, and literature have been among the most individualistic and impressive in the world.

The Buddha was born in approximately 563 B.C.—the date is controverted—in northeastern India. It was a period of dreams and intellectual excitement but also of conventional attitudes in religion and of an increasingly rigid caste system. The literature of

Buddhism did not materialize until some four centuries after the Buddha's death, and thus obviously cannot be said to be a precise record of his words. There is, however, no reason to doubt that the Buddhist scriptures contain an accurate embodiment of the Buddha's life and thought.

Siddhartha Gautama was the son of a rajah and, according to tradition, possessed great beauty and an incisive intellect. The world—pleasure, money, sensual experience, ease—was his. Indeed, one of his father's concerns was to keep him from any knowledge of the sorrows, cares, and fears of normal life—a particular concern, for at Gautama's birth it had been prophesied that he would be a fully Enlightened One, one who would care not for accession to his father's throne.

Gautama married a cousin when he was quite young. (Legend has it that he won his bride in a contest of arms, but it seems more likely that the marriage was arranged by the parents of the couple.) With his palaces and ready access to pleasures, with doting father and abundant dancing girls, he seemingly had everything a wealthy young man of his time might want. Yet, he soon tired of it, began to leave his palaces for journeys into the city where, from his chariot, he saw that others did not share his good fortune, that many were starving, others were ill, still others were dying. It was a revelation to the young man and it brought him to what Buddhists call the Great Renunciation. Following it, the prince departed from his palace, from his wife and newborn child, in the midst of the night, met a beggar, with whom he exchanged garments, and then went off into the forest.

Enlightenment did not come immediately. It was only after a period of studying with various holy men, of severe mortification of the body which brought him almost to the point of death, and of abandonment by many of his followers that Gautama became the Buddha. The Buddhist *Dhammapada* records:

> Not nakedness, nor matted hair, nor dust and dirt, nor sleeping on bare floors, nor squatting on the heels can purify a man who has not solved his doubts. But one who, though beautifully dressed, has a mind that is powerful and restrained, who is chaste, and who has abandoned all harm to human beings—he is indeed a Brahmin, ascetic, and monk.

Emaciated from fasting, Gautama finally ate, then sat down under a fig tree, the Bodhi tree, as it was to be called, near the bank of the Neranjara River, determined to remain there until he found an answer, achieved enlightenment. In time it came, a full cosmic consciousness. Only then did he become a Buddha, an Enlightened or Awakened Being.

For more than forty years he devoted himself to "showing the way," teaching that man must find the path to peace and knowledge through his own efforts. Or, as he said: "Within this very body, mortal as it is and only six feet in length, I do declare to you are the world and the origin of the world, and the ceasing of the world and the path that leads to cessation." Nirvana—the release from the idea of a separate "self" and from one's blind appetites—was the final goal. Illumination would come only through determination, "awareness" in thought and action, and an intense desire to abandon ego-centered patterns and behavior.

From the beginning, the Buddha stressed a "Middle Way" somewhere between extreme asceticism and self-indulgence, which he crystallized into a four-part formula that is known as the Four Noble Truths:

1) Suffering is universal.
2) It comes to men because they desire; they are self-centered, greedy, possessive, anxious for victory and gain.
3) These faults can, however, be understood and uprooted.
4) This can be accomplished by means of the Noble Eightfold Path, which involves thought, actions, and word.

The Eightfold Path is pivotal to Buddhism. It involves:

1) Right view. One must see clearly what is wrong.
2) Right purpose. One must reassess his values and desires and decide to rectify what is wrong.
3) Right speech. What, asked the Buddha, is right speech? "It is abstinence from lying speech, from backbiting and abusive speech, and from idle babble."
4) Right action. One must act in a way that is honest, pure, and peaceful.
5) Right livelihood. One's work must not make his adherence to the Eightfold Path impossible; nor may it cause suffering for others.
6) Right effort. One must strive to improve himself, to avoid evil, and to develop and preserve what is good.
7) Right awareness. The mind must be kept alert, vigilant, and constantly aware.
8) Right concentration. Through meditation one achieves a comprehension of reality, a "one-pointedness of mind," which enables the individual to attain a clarity in which Truth can be discerned.

"My teaching is pure and makes no distinction between noble and ignoble, rich and poor," said the Buddha. "My teaching is like water which cleanses all without distinction. My teaching is like fire which consumes all things between heaven and earth, great and small. My teaching is like the heavens; for there is ample room in it for all; for men and women, boys and girls, the powerful and the lowly."

For the Westerner, especially the Christian, with a belief in the "redemption" of souls, an emphasis on individuality and personality, Buddhism's rejection of ego is especially difficult to comprehend or accept. Yet, such Western philosophers as Bertrand Russell, William James, David Hume, and Arthur Schopenhauer have arrived at distinctly similar conclusions, which perhaps to some extent accounts for why many in the West, especially among the young, but certainly not confined to them, have found it more accessible and more appealing, more revelatory and satisfying, than might at first glance seem likely. Hume, voicing a concept that would not have been in the least alien to the Buddha, wrote:

> For my part, when I enter most intimately into what I call *myself,* I always stumble on some particular perception or other, of heat or cold, light or shade, love or hatred, pain or pleasure. I never can catch myself at any time without a perception and never can observe anything but the perception. . . . What we call the mind is nothing but a heap or bundle of different perceptions united together by certain relations.

Buddha had anticipated Hume by over two thousand years.

But, as indicated earlier, one should not push the similarities too far. For the Buddhist, theory or philosophy are not separate from an individual's acts. It is living by one's proclaimed philosophy, by what has been discovered to be True, that validates it. "The man who talks much of his teaching but does not practice it himself is like a cowman counting another's cattle," said the Buddha. "Like beautiful flowers full of color but without scent are the well-chosen words of the man who does not act accordingly."

Buddhism does not attempt to answer the unanswerable. ("The Buddha has no theories.") For the Buddha, silence—and how one could best live his own life—were preferable to speculation on metaphysics or "universals," and it is recorded that he once told a questioning monk: "Whether the dogma obtains that the world is eternal or that the world is not eternal, there still remain birth, old age, death, sorrow, lamentations, misery, grief, and despair—all the grim facts of human existence—for the extinction of which in the present life I am prescribing."

From this some have drawn the idea that Buddhism offers a philosophy that is primarily despairing, pessimistic, negative. But this is really a misinterpretation. "Nirvana," an old Sanskrit word, can be understood as meaning "extinction," but also, in the view of many Buddhists, as connoting that when Nirvana is attained what is extinguished is the self-centered life which intrudes upon, prevents, the *real* life.

In his *Invisible Anatomy,* Graham Howe writes: "In the course of their work, many psychologists have found, as the pioneer work of C. G. Jung has shown, that we are all near-Buddhists on our hidden side. . . . To read a little Buddhism is to realize that the Buddhists knew, two thousand five hundred years ago, far more about modern psychology than they have yet been given credit for. . . . We are now rediscovering the Ancient Wisdom of the East."

The extraordinary recent interest in and practice of Buddhism (especially in its Zen form) in the West has been paralleled by a revival in India, the land of its birth, which is reflected in attitudes toward the caste system, still to some degree extant, where the Untouchable no longer is consigned automatically to quite his former role. With its concern for creatures, *all* creatures, Buddhism could hardly acquiesce in the denigration inherent to the caste system and, although that system changes at a rate that still seems surprisingly slow, the Untouchable who becomes a Buddhist is today increasingly accepted.

Nirvana provides the major, perhaps the only, mystical idea of Buddhism, an idea that predominates to an extraordinary extent.

Apart from it, Buddhism is questioning, practical, skeptical. Nirvana passes beyond death, and the Buddha, whose ideas were in so many other ways revolutionary, accepted the traditional Indian belief in reincarnation. He did, however, believe in the possibility of what might be termed an "escape" from life's inevitable sorrow; that one who has attained the unitary consciousness could break that chain.

Tennyson suggested an attitude that has a considerable similarity to the concept of Nirvana:

> All at once, as it were out of the consciousness of individuality, individuality itself seemed to fade away into boundless being—the loss of personality (if so it were) seeming no extinction but the only true life.

And that is what Buddhism is—a Way of Life, a Way arrived at by a man, a man who was the recipient of mystical revelations, who refused to claim ultimate authority or to promise salvation by means of anything external to a process that could go on within the human mind, who repeatedly insisted, "One thing I teach, suffering and release from suffering."

In an introduction to a recent edition of F. L. Woodward's *Some Sayings of the Buddha,* the distinguished authority on Buddhism, Christmas Humphreys, suggests that Buddhism is, in fact, a "'do it yourself' religion."

Which would seem to make it a religion of neither East nor West, at least necessarily, a religion of humor, sensitivity, and practicality, one that, like most men, is involved in a search. As the Buddha said: "Change is inherent in all component things. Work out your own deliverance with diligence."

Unless indicated otherwise, all quotations that appear on the following pages have been attributed to the Buddha.

THE SOLITARY JOURNEY

Whoso the Faith and Wisdom hath attained—
His states of mind, well-harnessed,
    lead him on.
Conscience the pole, and Mind the yoke
    thereof,
And Heedfulness the watchful charioteer:
The furnishments of Righteousness, the Car:
Rapture the axle, Energy the wheels,
And Calm, yokefellow of the Balanced Mind:
Desirelessness the drapery thereof:
Goodwill and Harmlessness his weapons are,
Together with Detachment of the mind.
Endurance is the armour of the Norm,
And to attain the Peace that car rolls on.
'Tis built by self, by one's own
    self becometh—
This chariot, incomparable, supreme:
Seated therein the sages leave the world,
And verily they win the victory.

Short indeed is this life. This side of a hundred years it perishes. And, even if one live beyond, yet of decay he perishes at last.

It is from selfishness that people grieve. "Not lasting are possessions in this world: all this is liable to change." So seeing let not a man stay in his house. [Let him not cling to self or body.]

By death is put away even that of which one thinks "This is mine own." So seeing let not one devote himself to selfishness.

As when one awakes he sees no more him whom he met in a dream, even so one sees no more the beloved one who hath died and become a ghost.

The whole world is tormented by words
And there is no one who does without words.
But in so far as one is free from words
Does one really understand words.
                                        —Saraha

Not in the sky, not in the midst of the sea, nor anywhere on earth is there a spot where a man can be freed [from the consequences] of an evil deed.

The charitable man is loved by all; his friendship is prized highly; in death his heart is at rest and full of joy, for he suffers not trom repentance; he receives the opening flower of his reward and the fruit that ripens from it. Hard it is to understand: By giving away food, we get more strength; by bestowing clothing on others, we gain more beauty; by donating abodes of purity and truth, we acquire great treasures.

There is a proper time and a proper mode in charity; just as the vigorous warrior goes to battle, so is the man who is able to give. He is like a warrior, a champion strong and wise in action. Loving and compassionate, he gives with reverence and banishes all hatred, envy, and anger.

The charitable man has found the path of salvation. He is like the man who plants a sapling, securing thereby the shade, the flowers, and the fruit in future years.

Abandon thought and thinking and
    be just as a child.
Be devoted to your master's
    teaching, and the Innate will
    become manifest.
                          —Saraha

Not to follow after fools, but to follow
    after the wise:
The worship of the worshipful—this is the
    greatest blessing.

        *   *   *   *   *   *

Much learning and much science, and a
    discipline well learned,
Yea, and a pleasant utterance—this is the
    greatest blessing.

The support of mother and father, the
    cherishing of child and wife,
To follow a peaceful livelihood—this is the
    greatest blessing.

Giving of alms, the righteous life, to cheri
    kith and kin,
And to do deeds that bring no blame—thi
    is the greatest blessing.

        *   *   *   *   *   *

A heart untouched by worldly things, a he
    that is not swayed
By sorrow, a heart passionless, secure—t
    is the greatest blessing.
Invincible on every side, they who do
    these things
On every side they go to bliss—theirs is t
    greatest blessing.

The fool in doing ill knows not
    his folly:
His own deeds, like a fire,
    the fool consume.

He who offends the harmless
    innocent
Soon reaches one of the ten
    states of woe:

Sharp pain, disease, or bodily decay,
Grievous disaster, or a mind
    distraught,

Oppression by the king, or calumny,
Loss of relations, loss of all
    his wealth,

His house burned by a thunderbolt
    for fire:
At death, poor fool, he finds rebirth
    in Woe.

Enjoying the world of sense, one is undefiled
     by the world of sense.
One plucks the lotus without touching
     the water.
So the yogin who has gone to the root
     of things,
Is not enslaved by the senses although he
     enjoys them.

                                        —Saraha

Ye that are slaves of the "I," that toil in the service of self from morn to night, that live in constant fear of birth, old age, sickness, and death, receive the good tidings that your cruel master exists not. Self is an error, an illusion, a dream. Open your eyes and awake. See things as they are and you will be comforted. He who is awake will no longer be afraid of nightmares. He who has recognized the nature of the rope that seemed to be a serpent ceases to tremble. He who has found there is no "I" will let go all the lusts and desires of egotism.

Change is inherent in all component things.

Work out your own deliverance with diligence.

By faith you shall be free and go beyond the realm of death.

This world of men is attached to what it clings to, takes pleasure in what it clings to, delights in what it clings to. Since then this world is thus attached [to things] . . . a hard task it is for them [to grasp] . . . namely, the Originating of things by Dependence on Causes. A hard task it is for them to see the meaning of the fact that all activities may be set at rest, that all the bases of being may be left behind, the destruction of craving, Passionlessness, Cessation, which is [Nirvana].

Even as the moon makes light in black
    darkness,
So in one moment the supreme bliss
    removes all defilement.

—Saraha

Like everything else in nature, the life of man is subject to the law of cause and effect. The present reaps what the past has sown and the future is the product of the present. But there is no evidence of the existence of an immutable ego-being, of a self which remains the same and migrates from body to body. There is rebirth but no transmigration.

Is not this individuality of mine a combination, material as well as mental? Is it not made up of qualities that sprang into being by a gradual evolution? The five roots of sense-perception in this organism have come from ancestors who performed these functions. The ideas which I think came to me partly from others who thought them and partly they rise from combinations of the ideas in my own mind. Those who have used the same sense-organs and have thought the same ideas before I was composed into this individuality of mine are my previous existences; they are my ancestors as much as the *I* of yesterday is the father of the *I* of today, and the karma of my past deeds affects the fate of my present existence.

How blest in happy solitude
Is he who hears of truth the call!
How blest to be both kind and good,
To practice self-restraint to all!
How blest from passion to be free,
All sensuous joys to let pass by!
Yet highest bliss enjoyeth he
Who quits the pride of "I am I."

Impermanent and unstable are all
    conditioned things,
Essentially brittle, like an unbaked pot.
Like some borrowed article, like a town
    built on sand,
They last for a short while only.

These complexes are doomed to destruction,
Like plaster washed away by the
    rainy season,
Like sand on a river's bank.
They are subject to conditions, and their
    own-being is hard to get at.

Like the flame of a lamp are the complexes.
Suddenly it arises, soon it is doomed to stop.
Without any staying power they are, like air,
    or a mass of foam,
Unsubstantial and weak in themselves.

Complexes have no inner might, are void
        in themselves;
Rather like the stem of the plantain tree,
        when one reflects on them.
Like a mock show which deludes the mind,
Like an empty fist with which a child is teased.

Everything that is a complex event
Proceeds by way of causes and conditions,
And the events mutually cause and
        condition each other.
This fact is not understood by foolish people.

Rise from dreams and loiter not.
Open to truth thy mind.
Practice righteousness and thou
Eternal bliss shalt find.

By one's self the evil is done, by one's self one suffers; by one's self the evil is left undone, by one's self one is purified. The pure and the impure stand and fall by themselves, no one can purify another.

If one man conquer in a battle a thousand men, and if another conquer himself, he is the greatest of conquerors. One's own self conquered is better than the conquest of all other people; not even a god could change into defeat the victory of a man who is self-controlled and always calm.

The nature of decay is inherent in youth, the nature of sickness is in health, in the midst of life we are in death, so that now my complexion is no longer clear and translucent: all my limbs are loosed and wrinkled. Formerly my body was radiant, but now is seen a change of every organ—of sight, hearing, smelling, savouring, and body-feeling.

> Shame on thee, worthless age,
> That maketh colour fade!
> Thus the delightful form
> By age is trampled down.

> Who lives a hundred years
> Is nonetheless doomed to die.
> Naught can avoid Death's tread,
> That crusheth everything.

The life of mortals in this world is troubled and brief and combined with pain. For there is not any means by which those that have been born can avoid dying; after reaching old age there is death; of such a nature are living beings.

As ripe fruits are early in danger of falling, so mortals when born are always in danger of death.

As all earthen vessels made by the potter end in being broken, so is the life of mortals.

Both young and adult, both those who are fools and those who are wise, all fall into the power of death; all are subject to death.

Of those who, overcome by death, depart from life, a father cannot save his son, nor kinsmen their relations.

* * * * * *

People pass away and their fate after death will be according to their deeds.

He who seeks peace should draw out the arrow of lamentation, and complaint, and grief.

He who has drawn out the arrow and has become composed will obtain peace of mind; he who has overcome all sorrow will become free from sorrow, and be blessed.

By faith and virtue, energy and mind
In perfect balance, searching of the Norm,
Perfect in knowledge and good practices,
Perfect in concentration of your thoughts,
Ye shall strike off this multitude of woes.

Practice kindliness, for thereby all hate
will be abandoned.
Practice compassion, for thus will all
vexation be abandoned.
Practice sympathy, for thereby will all
aversion be abandoned.
Practice equanimity, for thereby will all
repulsion be abandoned.
Meditate on the ugly and so will lust
be abandoned.
Think about impermanence and then will
self-pride be abandoned.

Faith can cross the flood,
even as the master of the ship
    [sails across];
ever advancing in the conquest
    of sorrow,
Wisdom lands us on the
    Other Shore.
The wise man who lives by faith,
in virtue of his holy life enjoys
    unselfish bliss,
and casts off all shackles.
Faith lays hold of true Wisdom;
Religion leads to deliverance
    from Death;
from hearing comes knowledge,
which brings with it enlightenment;
faith with obedience is the path
    of Wisdom:
firmly persevering, a man finds
    escape from pain,
and is thus able to pass over
and escape the gulf of destruction.
    —Fa-Kheu-King-Tsu

They who yield to their desires
    Down the stream of craving swim:
As we see the spider run
    In the net himself hath spun.
Wise men cut the net and go
    Free from craving, free from woe.
Loose all behind, between, before:
    Cross thou to the other shore.
With thy mind on all sides free
    Birth and death no more shalt see.

Do not deceive, do not despise
Each other, anywhere.
Do not be angry, nor should ye
Secret resentment bear;
For as a mother risks her life
And watches o'er her child,
So boundless be your love to all,
So tender, kind, and mild.

Yea, cherish good will right and left,
All round, early and late,
And without hindrance, without stint,
From envy free and hate,
While standing, walking, sitting down,
Whae er you have in mind,
The rule of life that's always best
Is to be loving-kind.

The wise and thoughtful man
attacks his faults
One after other, momently,
In order due, and rubs them
all away,
E'en as a smith blows off the
silver's dross.
Just as the iron rust accumulates
Self-born, and eats itself away,
So with the man who sinneth:
day by day
His own deeds to destruction
lead him on.

If a traveler does not meet with one who is better or his equal, let him firmly keep to his solitary journey; there is no companionship with fools. Long is the night to him who is

awake; long is a mile to him who is tired; long is life to the foolish who do not know the true religion. Better than living a hundred years not seeing the highest truth is one day in the life of a man who sees the highest truth.

The man who talks much of his teaching but does not practice it himself is like a cowman counting another's cattle.

Not to be reached by going is world's end.
Yet is there no release for man from woe,
Unless ye reach world's end. Yea verily
He that is wise and lives the holy life,
He knows the world. He goeth to world's end.
Calmed is he, for he knows. He hankereth
Neither for this world nor for any world.

And what is birth? Whatever for this or that being in this or that class of beings is the conception, the birth, the descent, the production, the appearance of the khandhas, the acquiring of the sensory fields: this is called birth.

And what is becoming? There are these three becomings: sensuous becoming, fine-material becoming, immaterial becoming.

And what is grasping? There are four graspings: after sense-pleasures, after speculative view, after rite and custom, after the theory of self.

And what is craving? There are six classes of craving: for material shapes, sounds, smells, tastes, touches, and mental objects.

And what is feeling? There are six classes of feeling: feeling due to visual, auditory, olfactory, gustatory, physical, and mental impact.

And what is impression? There are six classes of impression: visual, auditory, olfactory, gustatory, physical, and mental.

And what is consciousness? There are six classes of consciousness: visual, auditory, olfactory, gustatory, physical, and mental consciousness.

And what is ignorance? Whatever is the unknowing in regard to suffering, its arising, its stopping, and the course leading to its stopping—this is called ignorance.

The world is afflicted with death and decay, therefore the wise do not grieve, knowing the terms of the world.

In whatever manner people think a thing will come to pass, it is often different when it happens, and great is the disappointment. Such are the terms of the world.

Faith is the wealth here best for man—by faith
the flood is crossed.

Decay is inherent in all component things,

but the truth will remain forever!

All acts of living become bad by ten things, and by avoiding the ten things they become good. There are three evils of the body, four evils of the tongue, and three evils of the mind.

The evils of the body are murder, theft, and adultery; of the tongue, lying, slander, abuse, and idle talk; of the mind covetousness, hatred, and error.

I exhort you to avoid the ten evils: Kill not, but have regard for life. Steal not, and do not rob; but help everybody to be master of the fruits of his labor. Abstain from impurity, and lead a life of chastity. Lie not, but be truthful. Speak the truth with discretion, fearlessly and in a loving heart. Invent not evil reports, and do not repeat them. Carp not, but look for the good sides of your fellow-beings, so that you may with sincerity defend them against their enemies. Swear not, but speak decently and with dignity. Waste not the time with gossip, but speak to the purpose or keep silence. Covet not, nor envy, but rejoice at the fortunes of other people. Cleanse your heart of malice and cherish no hatred, not even against your enemies; but embrace all living beings with kindness. Free your mind of ignorance and be anxious to learn the truth, lest you fall a prey either to skepticism or to errors. Skepticism will make you indifferent and errors will lead you astray so that you shall not find the noble path that leads to life eternal.

There are five meditations.

The first meditation is the meditation of love in which thou must so adjust thy heart that thou longest for the weal and welfare of all beings, including the happiness of thine enemies.

The second meditation is the meditation of pity, in which thou thinkest of all beings in distress, vividly representing in thine imagination their sorrows and anxieties so as to arouse a deep compassion for them in thy soul.

The third meditation is the meditation of joy in which thou thinkest of the prosperity of others and rejoicest with their rejoicings.

The fourth meditation is the meditation on impurity, in which thou considerest the evil consequences of corruption, the effects of wrongs and evils. How trivial is often the pleasure of the moment and how fatal are its consequences!

The fifth meditation is the meditation on serenity, in which thou risest above love and hate, tyranny and thraldom, wealth and want, and regardest thine own fate with impartial calmness and perfect tranquillity.

He who fills his lamp with water will not dispel the darkness and he who tries to light a fire with rotten wood will fail. And how can anyone be free from self by leading a wretched life if he does not succeed in quenching the fires of lust, if he still hankers after either worldly or heavenly pleasures. But he in whom self has become extinct is free from lust; he will desire neither worldly nor heavenly pleasures and the satisfaction of his natural wants will not defile him. However, let him be moderate, let him eat and drink according to the needs of the body.

Sensuality is enervating; the self-indulgent man is a slave to his passions and pleasure-seeking is degrading and vulgar.

But to satisfy the necessities of life is not evil. To keep the body in good health is a duty, for otherwise we shall not be able to trim the lamp of wisdom and keep our mind strong and clear. Water surrounds the lotus-flower, but does not wet its petals.

A man may dwell beside me,
and yet, being disobedient,
be far away from me.

The nature of the sky is
       originally clear,
But by gazing and gazing the sight
       becomes obscured.
Then when the sky appears
       deformed in this way,
The fool does not know that the
       fault's in his own mind.

Through fault of pride he does not
       see truth,
And therefore like a demon he
       maligns all ways.
The whole world is confused by
       schools of thought,
And no one perceives his
       true nature.

They do not perceive the true basis
       of mind,
For upon the Innate they impose a
       threefold falsification.
Where thought arises and where
       it dissolves,
There you should abide O my son.
                              —Saraha

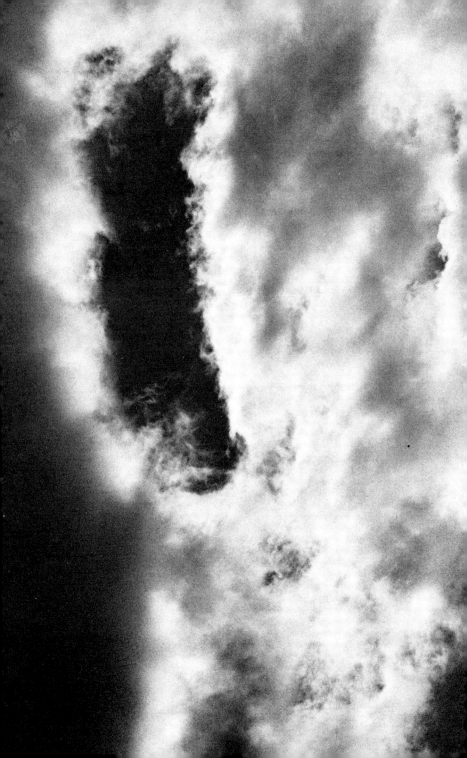

Truly the body is full of impurity and its end is the charnel house, for it is impermanent and destined to be dissolved into its elements. But being the receptacle of karma, it lies in our power to make it a vessel of truth and not of evil. It is not good to indulge in pleasures of the body, but neither is it good to neglect our bodily needs and to heap filth upon impurities. The lamp that is not cleansed and not filled with oil will be extinguished and a body that is unkempt, unwashed, and weakened by penance will not be a fit receptacle for the light of truth. Attend to your body and its needs as you would treat a wound which you care for without loving it. Severe rules will not lead the disciples on the middle path which I have taught. Certainly, no one can be prevented from keeping more stringent rules, if he sees fit to do so, but they should not be imposed upon anyone, for they are unnecessary.

The life of people in this world is short and intermingled with pain. Those who are born must sometime die. They are always in danger of death, just as ripe fruits are in danger of falling. In a world afflicted with death and decay wise people do not grieve. For they accept the rules of the world.

Believe nothing just because you have been told it, or it is commonly believed, or because it is traditional or because you yourselves have imagined it. Do not believe what your Teacher tells you merely out of respect for the Teacher. But whatsoever, after due examination and analysis, you find to be conducive to the good, the benefit, the welfare of all beings—that doctrine believe and cling to, and take as your guide.

And what is aging and dying? Whatever for this or that class of beings is aging, decreptitude, breaking up, hoariness, wrinkling of the skin, dwindling of the life-span, overripeness of the sense-faculties: this is called aging. Whatever for this or that being in this or that class of beings is the falling and deceasing, the breaking, the disappearance, the mortality and dying, the passing away, the breaking of the khandhas, the laying down of the body: this is called dying. This is called aging and dying.

I see no other single hindrance such as this hindrance of ignorance, obstructed by which mankind for a long time runs on and circles on.

Who harmeth him that doth no harm
And striketh him that striketh not,
Shall gravest punishment incur,
The which his wickedness begot.

Some of the greatest ills in life,
Either a loathsome dread disease,
Or dread old age, or loss of mind,
Or wretched pain without surcease,
Or conflagration, loss of wealth;
Or of his nearest kin he shall
See someone die that's dear to him,
And then he'll be reborn in hell.

A word spoken in wrath is the sharpest sword; covetousness is the deadliest poison; passion is the fiercest fire; ignorance is the darkest night.

Ignorance causes the ruin of the world. Envy and selfishness break off friendships. Hatred is the most violent fever, and the Buddha is the best physician.

Be ye lamps unto yourselves. Rely on yourselves and do not rely on external help.

Hold fast to the truth as a lamp. Seek salvation alone in the truth. Look not for assistance to anyone besides yourselves.

And how can a brother be a lamp unto himself, rely on himself only and not on any external help, holding fast to the truth as his lamp and seeking salvation in the truth alone, looking not for assistance to anyone besides himself?

Herein, let a brother, as he dwells in the body, so regard the body that he, being strenuous, thoughtful, and mindful, may, whilst in the world, overcome the grief which arises from the body's cravings.

While subject to sensations let him continue so to regard the sensations that he, being strenuous, thoughtful, and mindful, may, whilst in the world, overcome the grief which arises from the sensations.

And so, also, when he thinks or reasons, or feels, let him so regard his thoughts that being strenuous, thoughtful, and mindful he may, whilst in the world, overcome the grief which arises from the craving due to ideas, or to reasoning, or to feeling.

Those who shall be lamps unto themselves, relying upon themselves only . . . and seeking their salvation in the truth alone, and shall not look for assistance to anyone besides themselves, it is they who shall reach the very topmost height!

The man who plunges in the spate,
Flooding and turgid, swift of flow,
He, borne along the current's way,
How can he others help to cross?

As one who boards a sturdy boat
With oars and rudder well equipt,
May many others help to cross—
Sure, skillful knower of the means:

So the self-quickened love-adept,
Listener imperturbable,
By knowledge may help others muse,
The eager-eared adventurers.

Not nakedness, nor matted hair,
    nor filth,
Nor fasting long, nor lying on
    the ground,
Not dust and dirt, nor squatting
    on the heels,
Can cleanse the mortal that is
    full of doubt.

But one that lives a calm and
    tranquil life,
Though gaily decked—if tamed,
    restrained he live,
Walking the holy path in
    righteousness,
Laying aside all harm to
    living things—
True mendicant, ascetic,
    Brahmin he.

Assailed by death in life's last throes
On quitting all thy joys and woes
What is thine own, thy recompense?
What stays with thee when passing hence?
What like a shadow follows thee
And will Beyond thine heirloom be?

'Tis deeds, thy deeds, both good and bad;
Naught else can after death be had.
Thy deeds are thine, thy recompense;
They are thine own when going hence;
They like a shadow follow thee
And will Beyond thine heirloom be.

Let all then here perform good deeds,
For future weal a treasure store;
There to reap crops from noble seeds,
A bliss increasing evermore.

Practice kindliness, for thereby all hate
will be abandoned.
Practice compassion, for thus will all
vexation be abandoned.
Practice sympathy, for thereby will all
aversion be abandoned.
Practice equanimity, for thereby will all
repulsion be abandoned.
Meditate on the ugly and so will lust
be abandoned.
Think about impermanence and then will
self-pride be abandoned.

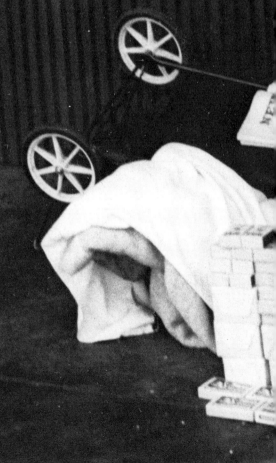

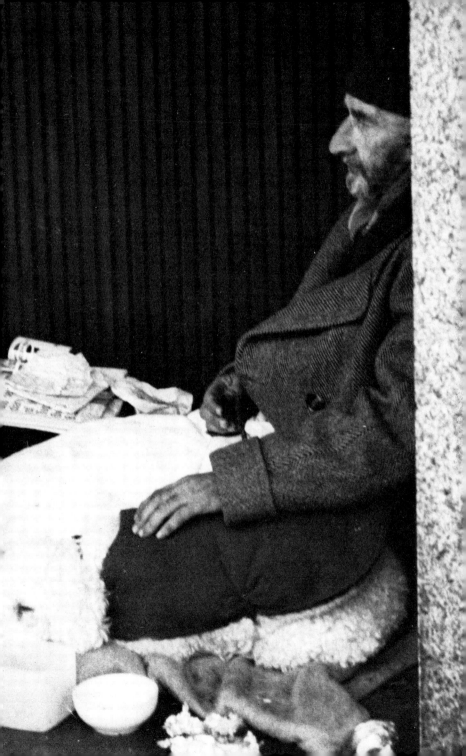

People are in bondage because they have not yet removed the idea of the ego. The thing and its quality are different in our thought, but not in reality. Heat is different from fire in our thought, but you cannot remove heat from fire in reality. You say that you can remove the qualities and leave the thing, but if you think your theory to the end, you will find that this is not so.

Is not man an organism of many aggregates? Are we not composed of various attributes? Man consists of the material form, of sensation, of thought, of disposition, and, lastly, of understanding. That which men call the ego when they say "*I* am" is not an entity behind the attributes; it originates by their cooperation.

There are two extremes which the man who has given up the world ought not to follow: the habitual practice, on the one hand, of self-indulgence which is unworthy, vain, and fit only for the worldly-minded, and the habitual practice, on the other hand, of self-mortification, which is painful, useless, and unprofitable.

Neither abstinence from fish or flesh, not going naked, nor shaving the head, nor wearing matted hair, nor dressing in a rough garment, nor covering oneself with dirt, nor sacrificing to Agni will cleanse a man who is not free from delusions.

That which ye sow, ye reap.
    See yonder fields!
The sesamum was sesamum,
    the corn
Was corn. The Silence and the
    Darkness knew!
So is a man's fate born.
He cometh, reaper of the things
    he sowed.

Good is attractive; evil is disgusting. A bad conscience is the most tormenting pain; deliverance is the height of bliss.

If a man lives a hundred years
and engages the whole of his time and
    attention
in religious offerings to the gods,
sacrificing elephants and horses and
    other things,
all is not equal to one act of pure love
    in saving life.

                    —Fa-Kheu-King-Tsu

Evil thought is the most dangerous thief; virtue is the most precious treasure. The mind takes possession of everything not only on earth, but also in heaven, and immortality is its securest treasure trove.

Though a person be ornamented with jewels the heart may have conquered the senses. The outward form does not constitute religion or affect the mind. Thus the body of a hermit may wear an ascetic's garb while his mind is immersed in worldliness. A man that dwells in lonely woods and yet covets worldly vanities is a worldling, while the man in worldly garments may let his heart soar high to heavenly thoughts. There is no distinction between the layman and the hermit if both have banished the thought of self.

How much confusion of thought comes from our interest in self and from our vanity when thinking "*I* am so great" or "*I* have done this wonderful deed"? The thought of your ego stands between your reason and truth; banish it, and then will you see things as they are. He who thinks correctly will rid himself of ignorance and acquire wisdom. The ideas "*I* am," "*I* shall be," or "*I* shall not be" do not occur to a clear thinker.